Squ Fair

by Francisco Garcia
illustrated by Jane McCreary

HOUGHTON MIFFLIN   BOSTON

Printed in China

ISBN 10: 0-618-88697-4
ISBN 13: 978-0-618-88697-5

15 16 17 18 19 20 0940 21 20 19 18 17 16
4500607556

There were all sorts of squares at the Square Fair. There were big squares, little squares, colorful squares, and plain squares.

Read • Think • Write How many sides does a square have?

Beth thought her square was the best of all. It was shiny and the color of gold. Beth hoped it might win a prize.

Read • Think • Write   How many vertices does a square have?

Beth put her square on the table.

Soon, it was time for the judge to look at all the squares. Beth was so excited! She jumped up when the judge got close.

Read • Think • Write How is a square different than a rectangle?

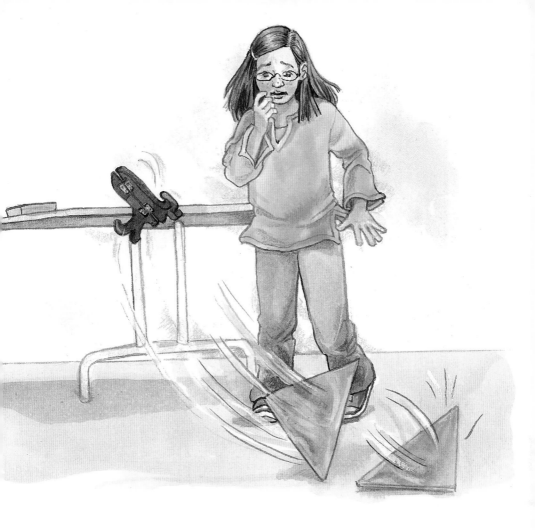

Beth bumped the table. Her gold square fell to the floor and broke. Beth was so sad. She picked up the two pieces and put them on the table.

Read • Think • Write What shape are the two pieces?

The judge looked carefully at the triangles.
"How clever!" she said. "You've made
a puzzle!"

Beth wasn't sure what the judge meant.

Read • Think • Write How many sides does a
triangle have?

"These triangles together make a square," said the judge. "You are a winner!"

Beth was so surprised!

Read • Think • Write   How many vertices does a triangle have?

Two in One

Show

Look at page 6. Draw a square. Show how it can be made of two shapes.

Share

Recognize Main Idea, Topic, and Supporting Details Talk about the picture on page 6. Tell how two shapes make one shape.

Write

Look at page 6. Write the name of the 2 shapes that make a square.